T0145021

My Hope Is Built

Rebuilding Hope After a Broken Relationship, Separation or Divorce

LORNA BROWN

Copyright © 2018 Lorna Brown.

All rights reserved. No part of this book may be used or reproduced by any means, graphic, electronic, or mechanical, including photocopying, recording, taping or by any information storage retrieval system without the written permission of the author except in the case of brief quotations embodied in critical articles and reviews.

Interior Image Credit: Shutterstock.com; 123rf.com

Scripture quotations marked (NLT) are taken from the Holy Bible, New Living Translation, copyright ©1996, 2004, 2015 by Tyndale House Foundation. Used by permission of Tyndale House Publishers, Inc., Carol Stream, Illinois 60188. All rights reserved.

Scripture taken from the King James Version of the Bible.

Scripture quotations are from the ESV® Bible (The Holy Bible, English Standard Version®), copyright © 2001 by Crossway, a publishing ministry of Good News Publishers. Used by permission. All rights reserved.

Holy Bible: The Contemporary English Version. 1995. Nashville: Thomas Nelson.

Scripture quotations taken from the Amplified® Bible (AMP), Copyright © 2015 by The Lockman Foundation Used by permission. www.Lockman.org

Scripture texts in this work are taken from the New American Bible, revised edition© 2010, 1991, 1986, 1970 Confraternity of Christian Doctrine, Washington, D.C. and are used by permission of the copyright owner. All Rights Reserved.

WestBow Press books may be ordered through booksellers or by contacting:

WestBow Press
A Division of Thomas Nelson & Zondervan
1663 Liberty Drive
Bloomington, IN 47403
www.westbowpress.com
1 (866) 928-1240

Because of the dynamic nature of the Internet, any web addresses or links contained in this book may have changed since publication and may no longer be valid. The views expressed in this work are solely those of the author and do not necessarily reflect the views of the publisher, and the publisher hereby disclaims any responsibility for them.

This book is a work of non-fiction. Unless otherwise noted, the author and the publisher make no explicit guarantees as to the accuracy of the information contained in this book and in some cases, names of people and places have been altered to protect their privacy.

ISBN: 978-1-9736-4327-2 (sc)
ISBN: 978-1-9736-4328-9 (e)

Library of Congress Control Number: 2018912642

Print information available on the last page.

WestBow Press rev. date: 11/08/2018

WestBow
PRESS®
A DIVISION OF THOMAS NELSON
& ZONDERVAN

For I will restore health unto thee, and I will heal thee of thy wounds, saith the LORD; because they called thee an Outcast.. Jeremiah 30:17 (KJV)

Psalms 66:16-17, 19B(NLT)

[16] Come and listen, all you who fear God,

and I will tell you what he did for me.

[17] For I cried out to him for help,

praising him as I spoke..He paid attention to my prayer. 19:b

"Tears, fears and jeers; He hears them all and responds with cheer".

CONTENTS

HOPE
SHATTERED

BROKEN PROMISES

O NO, THIS CANNOT BE
HE'S BREAKING ALL HIS PROMISES TO ME
O NO, THIS CANT BE TRUE
O LORD, WHAT WILL I DO

We make so many promises to one another before entering a marriage that when your spouse no longer cares enough to keep them or go out of his way to deliberately break them, the disappointment is numbing. It's the feeling of everything reeling out of control and helplessness like watching grains of sand slip through your fingers. Every broken promise becomes another piece of your broken heart. There is that gasp of "oh no", that suffocating feeling that you will never breathe again and if you do, perhaps you'll not have enough strength to finish that breath. I remember that about the time my marriage started falling apart, the pop singer Toni Braxton released her hit song "Breathe Again" promising to never breathe again if the lover never came back to her arms. The hook of the song was catchy, seemed like she was "Singing my life with her words" and I found myself many time singing along. But one day the Spirit of God in me rebuked me, "oh no, you can't sing that song for you shall breathe again". And I did, sometimes one painful second at a time, but I kept on breathing for unlike man God does not lie, he is not human, so he does not change his mind (See **Numbers 23:19 NLT**). Be strong my sister, you will not die; instead live. Breathe again; make up your mind to live to tell what the Lord has done. **(Psalms 118:17 KJV)**

Prayer: Father I thank you for every breath I breathe. I recognize that each one is a gift from you and it is not tempered by my circumstances. This will not suffocate me, this will not take my breath away, and this is not my last gasp. With your help Lord, I shall breathe again.

Numbers 23:19 (NLT)

God is not a man, so he does not lie.

> He is not human, so he does not change his mind.

Has he ever spoken and failed to act?

> Has he ever promised and not carried it through?

Psalms 118:17 (NLT)

I will not die; instead, I will live

> to tell what the LORD has done.

LET'S PRETEND

OUTSIDE I SMILE, INSIDE I'M DYING
O FATHER I CANT LET THEM SEE ME CRYING
SO HUSH MY BROKEN HEART
NOW DON'T START
PERHAPS IF WE PLAY THE ROLE, ACT THE PART
WE'LL WAKE UP AND FIND WE'RE ONLY DREAMING

When your marriage starts to fall apart, especially if it happens within a relatively short amount of time; mine was within months; you experience such shame and embarrassment. So you put on a face, a façade for your family, for the members of your congregation even your co-workers. You think maybe I can get this fixed before they find out what's happening and they will be no wiser. I can't let anyone see me crying, is a daily mantra, an every Sunday morning service requirement, just like my Bible. Broken heart don't you dare betray me, I can't let them see the tracks of my tears. But thank God there was one person I could turn to "But in my distress I cried out to the Lord; yes, I prayed to my God for help. He heard me from his sanctuary; my cry to him reached his ears". **Psalms 18:6 (NLT)**. I ruined many a pillow cases crying myself to sleep at nights, but I was comforted that my crying was not in vain for I was also crying to my heavenly Father. And I fell asleep laying on the breast of El Shaddai (the many breasted one) and in his everlasting arms. His left hand is under my head and his right hand doth embrace me. **(Songs of Solomon 2:6)**. As for the shame, very early on, I heard the Lord say, the enemy could not have my dignity; that was not up for grabs. My dear sister, your heavenly father sees and hears your cry. He sees you struggling with the embarrassment and losing your dignity is not an option. You are his child, you are in his care. Should you wake up tomorrow and find out the whole world knows your plight, it would still be alright. Walk tall, for the Lord is on your side and "…None who hope in me shall be ashamed" **Isaiah 49:23 (NABRE)**

Prayer: Lord, I am so glad that I don't have to pretend with you. I can lift my tear filled eyes to your face without shame and embarrassment. And on those days when I feel like looking down, you are the lifter up of my head. I take comfort in knowing that you are bottling up every tear. Thank you for walking with me. I will come out of this wilderness of shame and pain leaning on you my beloved. Through this veil of tears, I smile, knowing that the King of Kings is not ashamed to walk with me

Isaiah 61:7 (NLT) Instead of shame and dishonor, you will enjoy a double share of honor. You will possess a double portion of prosperity in your land, and everlasting joy will be yours.

Isaiah 49:23 (NLT) Kings and queens will serve you and care for all your needs. They will bow to the earth before you and lick the dust from your feet. Then you will know that I am the LORD. Those who trust in me will never be put to shame."

Psalms 146:3 (KJV) Put not your trust in princes, nor in the son of man, in whom there is no help.

HE LOVES ME, HE LOVES ME NOT..

O FATHER, PLEASE STOP THIS MADNESS
MY HEART CAN'T STAND ANYMORE SADNESS
HE'S GOING THROUGH THE DOOR
HE SAYS "I CANT LOVE YOU ANYMORE"
HIS EARS ARE DEAF TO MY HURT AND PAIN
HE IGNORES MY TEARS FALLING LIKE RAIN
O FATHER, I KNOW NOT WHAT TO DO
HOLD ME AND TELL ME YOU'LL SEE ME THROUGH

You think to yourself, maybe if I cry enough and beg enough something inside of him will be touched and he will stay. Seems like the man you remember falling in love with had a tender heart. And sometimes it seems like the tears and the begging did work, sometimes he did seem to try, but it would only last a day or two. You feel like a floppy rag doll, things are good one day, the pits the next. Will he come home tonight? Will he speak to me today and if he does will it only be with the civility reserved for strangers. You're worn out from the anxiety of will this be the day he leaves, always waiting for that final shoe to drop. And when he finally walks out the door and says I won't be back this time, your knees give way, like Raggedy Anne. You wonder where I will find the strength to go on. The answer- thy God. **Psalms 68:28 (KJV)** Thy God hath commanded thy strength: strengthen, O God, that which thou hast wrought for us. You have a reservoir of strength that God has prepared for you just for this season, just for this time. This does not surprise him, so he has already commanded your strength. He will see you through.

Prayer: Father, you are the strength of my life. A good thing too, for my strength is almost gone. I don't even have the strength to hold on to you. I need to lean hard on you today and feel your everlasting arms holding me all day long. The only consistent thing I can still count on is that you won't leave me. Please do cover me with your love. Thank you for hearing my cry when no one else does and for coming to my rescue.

Deuteronomy 33:12 (KJV) And of Benjamin he said, The beloved of the LORD shall dwell in safety by him; and the Lord shall cover him all the day long, and he shall dwell between his shoulders.

Deuteronomy 33:26-27(KJV) There is none like unto the God of Jeshurun, who rideth upon the heaven in thy help, and in his excellency on the sky. The eternal God is thy refuge, and underneath are the everlasting arms: and he shall thrust out the enemy from before thee; and shall say, Destroy them.

CRYING IN THE NIGHT

THE NIGHT IS LONG, I'M WRACKED WITH PAIN
MY PILLOWS ARE WET AND TEARSTAINED
STILL HE'S GONE, BUT YOU ARE HERE
CONSOLING ME, DISPELLING MY FEARS
WILL THIS NIGHT END, WILL MY EYES CEASE TO RAIN
"YES' YOU ANSWER; "THE MORNING WILL COME, THE SUNSHINE AGAIN

The nights are long and lonely now that he is not next to you. To be honest, there were times that you felt the same when he was there. But now you're not only lonely but alone. Your mind is screaming "I'm afraid of being alone". Is there an end to this? You think. Will I ever get pass this pain. Sobbing, your head's throbbing and sleep seems far away. At the same time worrying that without sleep, tomorrow your coworkers will certainly know something is wrong. Funny the trivial things we think and care about even in the midst of such pain and distress. So, here I am afraid in the night and fearful that day will come. But always it was the word of God that comforted me. Heavenly father was and is always there. Night or day, he was a constant. Hear David's heart in **Psalms 42:8 (KJV).** Yet the LORD will command his lovingkindness in the day time, and in the night his song shall be with me, and my prayer unto the God of my life. **Psalms 30:5 (KJV)** …weeping may endure for a night but joy comes in the morning. He will see you through the long night and don't fear the morning. There is hope in the morning. Each new day brings you closer to healing and wholeness. Until then accept the consolation of your Father God. Encourage yourself, **Psalms 42:3 (KJV).** Why art thou cast down, O my soul? and why art thou disquieted within me? hope thou in God: for I shall yet praise him, who is the health of my countenance, and my God.

Prayer: O God, I am afraid in the night and afraid for the morning. Still I hear you saying "fear not, for I am with you" and I look forward to the promise of joy in the morning. Hold me close till then. Hold me till the sun shines again and then hold me some more

Psalms 42:3 KJV. My tears have been my meat day and night, while they continually say unto me, Where is thy God?

Psalms 42:3 KJV. Why art thou cast down, O my soul? and why art thou disquieted within me? hope thou in God: for I shall yet praise him, who is the health of my countenance, and my God.

A WAR OF WORDS

FATHER, DID YOU HEAR WHAT SHE JUST SAID
DOESN'T SHE KNOW HOW IT HURTS
OR IS IT THAT SHE WISHES ME DEAD
EACH WORD IS A KNIFE, SEE MY BLOOD SPURT

SHE WEILDS HER TONGUE AS A WEAPON
LETTING THE BLOWS FALL WHERE THEY MAY
FATHER, YOU ARE MY ONLY PROTECTION
HEAR ME AND HELP ME O GOD I PRAY

YOU SAID NO WEAPON FORMED AGAINST ME WOULD PROSPER
YOU SAID YOU WOULD RIGHT EVERY WRONG
O, BE MY SHIELD MY PROTECTOR
HIDE ME FROM THIS STRIFE OF TONGUES

Seems like many people feel that they have the right to say something about what you're going through. Quickly lines get drawn and sides are taken. The battle begins and words are the weapons of choice. Some are said behind closed doors and repeated by those who mistakenly think they are doing you service by repeating. Others are deliberately said in earshot, just to make sure you get the message. Where do I go to find protection from these arrows filled with deadly poisons? **Psalms 31: 13-20 (KJV)** *For I have heard the slander of many: fear was on every side: while they took counsel together against me, they devised to take away my life.[14] But I trusted in thee, O LORD: I said, Thou art my God.[18] Let the lying lips be put to silence; which speak grievous things proudly and contemptuously against the righteous.[20] Thou shalt hide them in the secret of thy presence from the pride of man: thou shalt keep them secretly in a pavilion from the strife of tongues.* Run my sister! Run to the presence of the Lord! There is safety in his presence. Good thing about his presence you can be with him anywhere at any time. In a crowd or all by yourself, he will show up.

Prayer: O God, the words of the people are scary and they frighten me. But you have not given me a spirit of fear. Help me to hear you above the noise of tongues. I yearn for the quietness of your presence, to lean against you and breathe in the serenity of your company. O be still my soul, listen only for the sound of his voice. Peace be still. O Father, be it unto me according to your word and not the word of the enemy or my enemies.

<u>**Proverbs 18:10 (KJV)**</u>. The name of the LORD *is* a strong tower: the righteous runneth into it, and is safe

<u>**Psalms 56:3 (KJV).**</u> What time I am afraid, I will trust in thee.

ALONE AGAIN

EATING ALONE AGAIN
LISTENING TO MYSELF CHEW
I FEEL LIKE INK WITHOUT A PEN
A SPRING MORNING WITHOUT DEW

SPENDING THE EVENING ALONE AGAIN
NO ONE WITH ME, NOT EVEN A FRIEND
WATCHING THE CLOCK GO ROUND, AGAIN AND AGAIN
SIX OCLOCK, SEVEN OCLOCK, NINE, NOW TEN

FALLING ASLEEP ALONE AGAIN
JUST MY PILLOW, MY BIBLE. TEDDYBEAR AND ME
HERE COMES THE TEARS AGAIN
JUST LONGING FOR SOMEONE TO TOUCH AND HOLD ME

I'm getting off the bus on my way home from work, wondering what scenario I will meet tonight the cold silence of anger or the sad silence of being alone again. And when it was the latter, it brought a mixture of relief but disappointment at being alone again. I called a friend at 2 a.m. one morning just to cry out. Figured I couldn't do that too often, my friend would soon tire of me. But you Lord was always there. In the midst of my tears, was always the hulking, hovering, overshadowing understanding that you are here. I think David experienced lonely times; **Psalms 142: 4 (KJV)** "looked on my right hand, and beheld, but there was no man that would know me: refuge failed me; no man cared for my soul.⁵ I cried unto thee, O LORD: I said, Thou art my refuge and my portion in the land of the living." Daughter of God, just know that when you feel abandoned the Lord is holding you close. **Psalms 27:10 (NLT)** Even if my father and mother abandon me, the Lord will hold me close. Perhaps you are one of those, who have never lived alone. Always it was with your family, then perhaps a roommate. This time of separation is a scary time for you. But take comfort in the words of the Lord; **Isaiah 41:10 (NLT)** don't be afraid, for I am with you. Don't be discouraged, for I am your God.I will strengthen you and help you. I will hold you up with my victorious right hand.

Prayer: Father, Thank you that when no one is with me, I am not alone; for you are with me. Right now your presence is so tangible; I can hear you breathing on me. I will make it through today, for you are with me and I will sleep well tonight for you are with me.

<u>**Isaiah 41:13 (KJV)**</u> For I the LORD thy God will hold thy right hand, saying unto thee, Fear not; I will help thee.

<u>**Psalms 46:7 (KJV)**</u>. The LORD of hosts *is* with us; the God of Jacob *is* our refuge. Selah.

PLEASE TAKE ME WITH YOU

MY HEART BREAKS AS I WATCH HIM DRESS
KNOWING IT'S NOT FOR ME, BUT SOMEONE ELSE

I WISH THINGS WERE LIKE THEY USED TO BE
I WISH HE WOULD SAY COME WITH ME

BUT HE WALKS OUT THE DOOR, HIS SCENT
STILL FRESH ON MY MIND
HE GAVE NOT A SECOND THOUGHT
TO LEAVING ME BEHIND

Part of the joy of courtship is the amount of time spent together. The simplest activity became a momentous occasion because we were together. Now watching him go through the door without me is devastating. It means that he will be making memories that do not include me and this by choice. I want so much to be with him and he seems determined to forget me. Sometimes I feel like he is trying to erase me as if I never was. The weight of the disappointment crushes my soul But I am comforted by the psalmist **Psalms 34:18 (ESV)** " **The** Lord is near to the brokenhearted and saves the crushed in spirit. Are you feeling crushed? Perhaps he has not actually said "forget you" but his every action clearly states it, or maybe he has said those words. Take comfort the Lord is near and he will lift that crushing weight from your heart. If as Isaiah tells us that even mothers may forget their child, it comes as no surprise that man may forget us, but says the Lord "I will not forget you". No matter how many loves leave you behind, the Lord your God will never leave you behind.

Prayer: Father, help me to know that though all may leave me, you never will. These days, I'm often out of sight and out of mind of the one I love. But, at this moment when I am feeling neglected and left out, I'm thankful that you are mindful of me, that I am never out of your sight or mind. I want to be with you and more important, you want to be with me. Thank you God, the Comforter abides with me

Isaiah 49:15-16 (ESV) "Can a woman forget her nursing child, that she should have no compassion on the son of her womb? Even these may forget, yet I will not forget you. Behold, I have engraved you on the palms of my hands; your walls are continually before me

LIGHTS OUT

THE LIGHT IN YOUR EYES HAS GONE OUT
IT USED TO SAY I LOVE YOU WITHOUT A DOUBT
BUT NOW, I SEE I'M NO LONGER THE APPLE OF YOUR EYE
ANYDAY NOW YOU WILL BE SAYING GOODBYE

Eyes that used to say I love you, now when I look into them I see disgust, I see hurt, I see mistrust. I see eyes that say I'm leaving. I longed to see the first fires that burned in his eyes for me, but that was not to be. Instead I woke up each day wondering if this would be the last day I would see him in our home or should I say place. For it had become only a place where we sheltered, no longer our home. So much had come between us and our love for each other; we were separated even before he moved out.

Prayer: Thank you Lord, that no matter what, your eyes always say "I love you" though I have disappointed you time and again, still in your eyes I see compassion. Help me today to look beyond the cold eyes of the one I love and see your eyes; full of warmth and invitation to come and rest in you. God, You are my home, You are my shelter in this weary land of marital distress. I will dwell in you, thank you for being my safe place.

Romans 8:38-39 (ESV). For I am sure that neither death nor life, nor angels nor rulers, nor things present nor things to come, nor powers, nor height nor depth, nor anything else in all creation, will be able to separate us from the love of God in Christ Jesus our Lord.

Isaiah 54:6 (ESV). For the LORD has called you like a wife deserted and grieved in spirit, like a wife of youth when she is cast off, says your God

PLEASE BELIEVE ME

MY LOVE, I CANT BELIEVE YOU THINK I'VE LIED
I CANNOT BELIEVE HOW QUICKLY YOUR LOVE DIED
DO YOU REALLY BELIEVE I LED YOU DOWN THIS PATH
AND THAT I AM DESERVING OF YOUR BITTER WRATH
KNOW THIS MY LOVE, I HAVE ALWAYS BEEN TRUE
AND I WILL ALWAYS BE DEVOTED TO YOU

You must know by now that the old adage "sticks and stones may break my bones, but words can never harm me" is not truth. One of the enemy's best loved tools is to use innocently said words or scenarios to create lies and mistrust. Satan is the father of lies and deception. It breaks the heart when you are accused of lying when deep in your heart you know that you have told nothing but the truth and the frustration is that there is no way to prove it and you know that if you were in the accuser's shoe you would think you were lying too. How many tears have you shed looking for vindication, hoping your husband would believe that you have not betrayed his trust or set out to hurt him? The lies of the enemy reconstructing your words in his ears, filling his mind with lies spoken by others who mistakenly feel they must take sides stack up like mountains too difficult to surmount. Wearily, you ask yourself and God, does he hear me, does anyone hear me, and does anyone believe me? Take comfort in God's truth. He knows the truth. **Psalms 139:4 (ESV)** Even before a word is on my tongue, behold, O LORD, you know it altogether. The one who knows the truth is also the one who never lies," and he will bring vindication **Psalms 135:14 (ESV)** For the LORD will vindicate his people and have compassion on his servants.

Prayer: Father, I find myself in a snare of accusation and the more I struggle to get out the more I feel trapped. I'm too tired to struggle anymore. Please just let me rest in you, for you alone know all my heart and my deeds. Help me to forgive those who trespass against me and let no root of bitterness grow in my heart. I am putting my trust in you and I know that I will not be ashamed. I trust you to keep my mind in perfect peace. I trust you to free me from webs of lies. I trust you to help me to trust others again and not let today's "sticks and stones" hinder your plans for my beautiful tomorrow. Thank you Father, you are faithful and true.

Psalms 17: 3 (CEV). You know my heart, and even during the night you have tested me and found me innocent. I have made up my mind never to tell a lie.

HOPE

THEN HE

THEN THUNDER
THEN LIGHTENING
FOUNDATIONS CRUMBLING
THEN ONLY THE SOUND OF RUSHING WATERS
THEN ONLYTHE HEARTBEAT OF MY FEARS
THEN NOTHING

THEN A MIGHTY VOICE
THEN A STREAM OF LIGHT
AN EVERLASTING ARM
THEN ONLY THE SOUND OF A RIVER OF PEACE
THEN ONLY THE STILLNESS OF WINDS THAT CEASED
THEN HE

*(He sent from above, he took me, he drew me out of many waters. **Psalms 18:16 KJV**)*

HOPE

"..He came to himself..." I love this excerpt from the parable of the prodigal son. I feel like it describes the way I felt when the realization came to me that I am God's child and he cares for me in the midst of it all and that he is looking for me to hold me and to heal me and restore me. I have hope; it would not always be like this. I lost my self in the whirlwind of marital upheaval and God's hope found me and pulled me back to him and that led me back to me. I once was lost, but now I'm found. God's hope showed me the way home, the way back to wholeness. It didn't happen overnight, but he patiently, gently and lovingly guided me. He will do the same for you. Look to him, he has opened a path for you to come to yourself and be made whole

LIGHT ON MY PATH

MY LORD WHAT IS THIS PATH I SEE
IS THAT REALLY YOU BECKONING TO ME
ARE ALL THOSE PROMISES REALLY MINE?
PRECEPT UPON PRECEPT, LINE UPON LINE
FEAR NOT MY HEART, NO LONGER GROPE
AWAKE, AWAKE, THERE IS HOPE.

Gradually there was an awakening in my heart; it was like the first streaks of light after midnight. **Psalms 119:105 (KJV) Thy word is a lamp unto my feet, and a light unto my path.**, I started to hope again. I meditated in the word of God and I found hope in them. I found hope in his promises. **Psalms 42:11King (KJV)** why art thou cast down, O my soul? and why art thou disquieted within me? hope thou in God: for I shall yet praise him, who is the health of my countenance, and my God. My situation had not change, but the light of God's word was changing me, helping me to see that life was worth living and living abundantly. It may be that your situation will not change, but know this that God is not through with you. You are still his child and he will see you through. Hear him calling your name through the darkness of your troubles. Your days of mindless groping are over, he is with you. **Isaiah 43: 1-2 (KJV)** But now thus saith the Lord that created thee, O Jacob, and he that formed thee, O Israel, Fear not: for I have redeemed thee, I have called thee by thy name; thou art mine. When thou passest through the waters, I will be with thee; and through the rivers, they shall not overflow thee: when thou walkest through the fire, thou shalt not be burned; neither shall the flame kindle upon thee.

Prayer: Father, I hear you calling me out of the darkness. Thank you, I feel hope and faith rising in me, telling me you have prepared a brighter day for me. I am weary, but you are the strength of my life and I will make it to that brighter day, leaning on your everlasting arms.

2 Samuel 22: 29 KJV. For thou *art* my lamp, O LORD: and the LORD will lighten my darkness.

Psalms 112:4 KJV. Unto the upright there ariseth light in the darkness: *he is* gracious, and full of compassion, and righteous.

I HAVE A SONG

YOU CAN SING IN THE STORM, I'M LEARNING AT LAST
NO NEED TO WAIT TILL THE CLOUDS ARE PAST
THE LORD IS MY SONG, HE PUTS MY HEART TO FLIGHT
I CAN SING IN THE GLOOMIEST AND DARKEST OF NIGHT

As I am writing this, my city is in the midst of a winter storm; but I am safe inside. Marital issues can seem like a winter storm. Cold, icy and dreary; but in the midst of the storm, I came to realize that I am safe. I am safe in my heavenly father and in his arms I feel the cold melting away. The gloom is giving way to a song. Maybe you have been praying and crying to the Lord about your situation for some time now and it looks and feels like nothing has changed. Be still a while and listen to your heart. If you listen, you will hear the sound of a song beginning to rise out of and in the midst of your storm. Jehovah is giving you his song. **Psalms 42:8 (KJV)** Yet the Lord will command his lovingkindness in the day time, and in the night his song shall be with me... Let your spirit and your hopes rise with that song. **<u>Isaiah 12: 2 (KJV)</u>** Behold, God is my salvation; I will trust, and not be afraid: for the Lord Jehovah is my strength and my song; he also is become my salvation.

Prayer: Father, please give me ears to hear what the Spirit is saying. I want to hear the song that you have put in my heart for this night season. I want to hear the hope that your still small voice is whispering to me. Thank you Lord, for singing your songs of deliverance over me. Be still my soul while I sing along with my deliverer.

Psalms 32:7 (KJV)

Thou art my hiding place; thou shalt preserve me from trouble; thou shalt compass me about with songs of deliverance. Selah.

HE GAVE ME SOUND MIND

MY HEART WAS SHATTERED, MY MIND WAS TOO
BUT YOU GAVE ME A SPIRIT OF LOVE, POWER AND SOUND MIND TOO
MY SPIRIT WAS BROKEN, MY STRENGTH ALL GONE
BUT I STILL HAD YOUR PROMISE "NEVER ALONE"
YOU SPENT THE NIGHT, NO MATTER HOW LONG
YOU TOOK THE SPIRIT OF HEAVINESS AND GAVE ME A SONG
ALL THE WHILE YOU WERE MENDING AND MOLDING
AND TEACHING MY HEART TO SING

This experience, watching my marriage fail within months has been mind-blowing and heart shattering. Really thought I would lose my mind over this and for sure the enemy threatened it all the time. He would on occasions point me to examples of others who unfortunately didn't survive life crises such as mine. But God.. God gave me the word in **2 Tim 1:7 KJV** For God hath not given us the spirit of fear; but of power, and of love, and of a sound mind. That word was my preservation. But not only was he preserving my mind, he was doing a process of exchange in me. He gave me beauty for ashes, the oil of joy for mourning, the garment of praise for the spirit of heaviness. He bound up my broken heart. He will do the same for you. Pay no mind to the enemy's threats. Focus instead on the trade that God is doing in your heart and life as David described in **Psalms 30:11-12 (AMP)** You have turned my mourning into dancing for me; You have taken off my sackcloth and clothed me with joy. That my soul may sing praise to You and not be silent. O Lord my God, I will give thanks to You forever.

Prayer: Father, you are the master potter. I bring to you every splintered fragment of me and I trust you to put me together again. Better than ever, double for my trouble. I thank you for preserving my mind. You have kept me one day at a time, sometimes one minute at a time. I will sing your praise in the midst of the congregation that others may know of your wonderful kindness. That they may know of your faithfulness in the night and your lovingkindness that greeted me in the mornings.

Isaiah 61: 1-3 (KJV)

The Spirit of the Lord GOD is upon me; because the LORD hath anointed me to preach good tidings unto the meek; he hath sent me to bind up the brokenhearted, to proclaim liberty to the captives, and the opening of the prison to them that are bound;

To proclaim the acceptable year of the LORD, and the day of vengeance of our God; to comfort all that mourn;

To appoint unto them that mourn in Zion, to give unto them beauty for ashes, the oil of joy for mourning, the garment of praise for the spirit of heaviness; that they might be called trees of righteousness, the planting of the LORD, that he might be glorified.

HOPE

HOPE IS THE ANCHOR WHEN LIFE'S WAVES ARE TOO STRONG
IT IS THE ROPE TO HOLD ON TO, WHEN LIFE IS QUICKSAND
HOPE IS THE SUNLIGHT RIGHT AFTER THE RAIN
IT'S DAWN AFTER A LONG NIGHT, THE HEALING AFTER THE PAIN
HOPE IS THAT WHICH I CANNOT SEE
BUT I KNOW MY FATHER HAS IN STORE FOR ME
HOPE IS A SONG RISING OUT OF THE DARK
SOARING EVER UPWARD, IT'S VOICE AS SWEET AS A LARK

As we are going through our circumstances and situations we can get used to waking up every day and living with dread and trepidation. This is not our heavenly father's desire for us. Instead he calls us to a life of hope and anticipation even in the midst of our troubles. So amidst it all we must get the right perspective. Remember how and where he has positioned us. We are placed above and not beneath **(Deut. 28:13 KJV)**. we are seated with Christ in heavenly places **(Eph. 2:6 KJV)**. Be determined to stay in your God given position. Don't let this crisis move you, hold on to hope. **Psalms 31:24 (KJV)** Be of good courage, and he shall strengthen your heart, all ye that hope in the Lord.

We have this

HOPE

as an anchor for the soul

Hebrews 6:19

Prayer: Father, today I turn to hope in you as my refuge. Right now, things feel so out of control and all I hold dear seems to be drifting away; hope in you is my only anchor. Help me to see that I am secured in you and nothing can unfasten me from you steadfast love and the plans you have for me

Psalms 30:5 (KJV). For his anger endureth but a moment; in his favour is life: weeping may endure for a night, but joy cometh in the morning.

Hebrews 6:18-19 (KJV) That by two immutable things, in which it was impossible for God to lie, we might have a strong consolation, who have fled for refuge to lay hold upon the hope set before us: Which hope we have as an anchor of the soul, both sure and steadfast, and which entereth into that within the veil;

RESTORER

I THOUGHT LIFE WAS OVER
AND LIFE LONG FRIENDS GONE
BUT HIS LOVE BECAME A BANNER
HE, THE REJECTED, THE CHIEF CORNERSTONE
HE SAID "I AM THE RESSURECTOR"
ALL WILL BE RESTORED

MY LIMBS WERE WEAK AND FEEBLE
CONFUSION FILLED MY FACE
IN FRONT OF MY ENEMIES HE MADE FOR ME A TABLE
HE SAID "CHILD, BEHOLD AMAZING GRACE"
ALL WILL BE REPLACED

The stress of a marriage gone wrong or going wrong touches so many areas of our lives. Our emotions, health even other relationships are affected. Not only is there the worry of can this marital relationship be restored; you wonder where are friends gone, will they come again? Will this have a lasting effect on my health and emotions? It is possible to feel like the prophet Isaiah's description of Israel "From the sole of the foot even unto the head there is no soundness in it; but wounds, and bruises, and putrefying sores: they have not been closed, neither bound up, neither mollified with ointment." **Isaiah 1:6 (KJV).** Understandable if no one wanted to come near that!! But God. "For I will restore health to you and I will heal your wounds, says the Lord, because they have called you an outcast saying: This is Zion; no one seeks her and no one cares for her" **Jeremiah 30:17 (AMP).** Our heavenly father the restorer comes near and he repairs and he rebuilds. "He restoreth my soul.. **Psalms 23:3 (KJV)**

Prayer: Father God, today I feel so torn on the inside, that I physically ache. Heavenly cornerstone please let me rest in and on you. Let your grace abound to all my weak places and strengthen me. I know that if I let you repair me, rebuild me, I shall be well again. I shall be whole again. Restorer, I place my life in your hands, all of me; spirit soul and body. Thank you Lord, for remaking this broken shattered jar of clay into a vessel of grace.

Isaiah 54:4 KJV. Fear not; for thou shalt not be ashamed: neither be thou confounded; for thou shalt not be put to shame: for thou shalt forget the shame of thy youth, and shalt not remember the reproach of thy widowhood any more.

Joel 2:25 KJV. And I will restore to you the years that the locust hath eaten, the cankerworm, and the caterpillar, and the palmerworm, my great army which I sent among you.

Jeremiah 31:4 KJV Again I will build thee, and thou shalt be built, O virgin of Israel: thou shalt again be adorned with thy tabrets, and shalt go forth in the dances of them that make merry.

Isaiah 62:4 KJV. Thou shalt no more be termed Forsaken; neither shall thy land any more be termed Desolate: but thou shalt be called Hephzibah, and thy land Beulah: for the LORD delighteth in thee, and thy land shall be married

ENTRANCE

SOMETIMES I WISHED I COULD CLOSE IT TO ALL
DROP ALL THE WINDOWS AND BUILD A WALL
CLOSE OUT THE SORROW, CLOSE OUT THE PAIN
THE NOISE OF THE THUNDER, THE SOUND OF THE RAIN

THEN I REMEMBER, THAT THIS HEART OF MINE
WILL ALWAYS HEAL IF I GIVE IT TIME
AND IF I OPEN THE SHUTTERS AND FLING OPEN THE DOORS
LOVE WILL COME GENTLY HOME ONCE MORE

The impact of my marriage failing left me feeling like an empty house that had been swept clean of persons and furniture. The waves of pain and hurt had left such a void in my heart; it seems the only thing left was the echoing sound of my grief as it bounced against the bruised walls of my soul. My survival instinct said shut down and let nothing or anyone come near this house again. Maybe if I brick walled the door to my heart for good, I could avoid ever feeling this way again. But houses are built for habitation or they are without purpose. My heart was made to love and to close it down would not only mean love would not come in, it would not flow out. I was made to love. To love God, to love me and to love others as myself is my purpose. All that God desires for me and from me flows from that purpose. I could not let fear of heartache take that from me as well. So I decided to trust my heart's protection to my heavenly father. I trust him to always be there in joy or pain. When all else leaves, the Holy Spirit, the Comforter abides. **Isaiah 12:2 (KJV)** Behold, God is my salvation; I will trust, and not be afraid: for the LORD JEHOVAH is my strength and my song; he also is become my salvation.

Song of Solomon 5:2 KJV I sleep, but my heart waketh: it is the voice of my beloved that knocketh, saying, Open to me, my sister, my love, my dove, my undefiled: for my head is filled with dew, and my locks with the drops of the night.

Prayer: Lord Jesus, you came to the earth to bring love to a world that would reject you and crucify you, yet even on the cross you opened your heart of love and said father forgive them. I want to be like you. Help me to open my heart again, to trust again with confidence that you will always be there to help me when that love is not reciprocated. Thank you that I can always depend on your love to sustain me and to fill up the empty places of my heart.

Song of Solomon 2:10-13. KJV. My beloved spake, and said unto me, Rise up, my love, my fair one, and come away. For, lo, the winter is past, the rain is over and gone; The flowers appear on the earth; the time of the singing of birds is come, and the voice of the turtle is heard in our land; The fig tree putteth forth her green figs, and the vines with the tender grape give a good smell. Arise, my love, my fair one, and come away.

HE

Patiently he watched and waited
She sought refuge in others
Spent time in other's arms

Patiently he watched this vessel that he created
Become broken and battered
Become ill-shaped and scarred

Patiently he watched this picture that he had painted
Become stripped and tattered
Become faded and marred

Patiently he watched her lovers retreated
She was beaten and shattered
She was alone and scared

..then..

Patiently he stooped and with hands that once waited
He gave her love like no other
He gave her peace and rest
Patiently he molded and created her again

ABOUT THE AUTHOR

Within months of getting married, Lorna's marriage was over. The pain, embarrassment and emptiness so overwhelming she thought she would not get through it. The lies of the enemy were constantly in her ears, particularly saying that she would lose her mind. But God gave a word that sustained her "For God hath not given us a spirit of fear, but of power and of love, and of a sound mind" (2 Timothy 1:7 KJV). She is thankful for the nights she fell asleep because she knew he was holding her hand and she was resting on the breast of the EL Shaddai. Thankful for the many mornings He got her out of bed and took her through the day in his strength alone. Today she is called on to preach and teach the word at conferences, conventions, retreats and serves as an Associate Pastor. Her testimony is "I am as a wonder unto many; but thou art my strong refuge." (Psalms 71:2 KJV).

Printed in the United States
By Bookmasters